The Floweret: A Gift Of Love

Anna Maria Wells

0

THE

FLOWERET.

A

GIFT OF LOVE.

By ANNA MARIA WELLS.

A simple flower to you I bring, —
In solitude it grew :
Accept the humble offering, —
I gathered it for you.

———

BOSTON:
WILLIAM CROSBY AND COMPANY.
1842.

CONTENTS.

	Page.
OVER THE BROOK	5
SWISS CHILDREN	8
LITTLE GIRLS	11
THE HUMMING BIRD	13
ROVER	16
THE BUTTERFLY	18
ELIZABETH AND ISABEL	20
MAMMA	22
TIED TO A CHAIR	25
THE MOUSE	27
THE BOY AND THE ROBIN	30
LUCY	33

CONTENTS.

	Page.
THE NEW YEAR	35
A, B, C	39
THE FLY	41
MISS NELLY	42
ELLEN TO HER COUSIN ANNA	43
ANNA'S ANSWER	52
THE FLY AND THE RAIN-DROP	62
THE STORY OF LITTLE SARAH	67

THE FLOWERET.

―――――

OVER THE BROOK.

Over the brook to Grandmamma's,
Over the brook, little boy ;
   The flowers are sweet,
   Beneath our feet,
We'll sing as we go, for joy.

▲

Over the brook to Grandmamma's,
The afternoon is fair;
    For butter-cups gay,
    Don't stop by the way,
'T is high time we were there.

Over the brook to Grandmamma's,
And down by the greenwood tree;
    In a pleasant spot
    Is our Grandmamma's cot,
And a dear old lady is she.

Over the brook to Grandmamma's,
She is looking for us, I know;
    Her table is spread
    With honey and bread,
And milk from the brindled cow.

Over the brook to Grandmamma's,
It is but a few steps more ;
　　Already I see
　　The cot and the tree,
And Grandmamma sits at the door.

Over the brook to Grandmamma's,
A mile and more we 've been ;
　　She opens the gate,
　　That we need not wait ;
She longs to let us in.

Over the brook to Grandmamma's,
And a kiss for you and for me ;
　　The journey is past,
　　We 're here at last,
And who so happy as we !

SWISS CHILDREN.

I saw a little Swiss girl,
  As home from church I came;
Her clothes were coarse, but whole and clean —
  The little girl was lame.

Upon her head no bonnet,
  Nor covering she wore;
Her hair behind was braided down,
  And smoothly combed before.

She came from out the same church
  Where I had been at prayer;
I oft before had noticed her,
  How quiet she was there.

For all she limped so sadly,
  'T was half a mile and more
She came, this little Swiss girl,
  From home to our church door.

I often walked behind her,
  Along her homeward way ;
And many words of kindness thought,
  That I should like to say.

Her older brother helped her,
  She scarce could go alone ;
I listened as he talked to her,
  How gentle was his tone.

They spoke in their own language,
  By me not understood ;
And yet I knew these children were
  Affectionate and good.

A gentle look, a kind tone,
   Can ne'er mistaken be ;
And let me meet them where I may,
   They will be dear to me.

LITTLE GIRLS.

Why are little girls, I pray,
Like the *birds* upon the spray ?
Why are little girls like *flowers*,
Shining in the summer hours ?
Why are little girls like *bees*,
Sucking honey where they please ?

Ever prattling merry words,
Little girls are like the *birds* ;
Full of life, and full of song,
Skipping, hopping, all day long.

Fresh and gay at morning hours,
Little girls are like the *flowers* :
Dews on rosy leaf appear,
On the rosy cheek a tear ;

Soon there comes a smiling ray,
Chasing dew and tear away.

Girls, like *bees*, find something sweet
In every opening flower they meet;
On, from joy to joy, they range,
Every minute brings a change.

When good nature lights the features,
Little girls are pleasant creatures;
Fluttering, blooming, busy, free, —
Like the *bird*, the *flower*, the *bee*.

THE HUMMING BIRD.

Anna, with a smiling face,
　　Came from the garden bowers,
And brought, to put in mother's vase,
　　An apron full of flowers.

She chose sweet pinks and roses red,
　　Lilies and larkspur blue ;
" I 'll paint a bunch like this," she said,
　　And held it up to view.

The work began — and all the while
　　Her busy brush was glancing,
Her mother looked, with pleasant smile,
　　To see the flower advancing.

A3

But suddenly a noise was heard,
  And Anna quick upstarted ;
A lovely little humming bird
  Straight through the window darted.

With outstretched arm and eager hand,
  All round and round she chased him ;
Caught him, and quickly on the stand,
  Beneath a tumbler, placed him.

And there his little wings he beat
  Against the tumbler o'er him,
And tried to reach the roses sweet
  That bloomed so bright before him.

At first, when Anna saw the same,
  She laughed with glad surprise ;
But then a thought of sadness came,
  And tears were in her eyes.

It pained her tender heart to see
  The dear bird struggling so ;
" He wants among the flowers to be —
  Mother, I 'll let him go."

" I 'm sure I should have cried if you
  Had kept me in to-day ;
And humming birds love freedom too ; —
  There, darling, fly away."

ROVER.

Old Rover is the finest dog
   That ever ran a race ;
His ear so quick, his foot so fleet,
   And such an honest face.

His eyes are brown as hazlenuts,
   His hair is dark and curly ;
He scuds along the dewy grass,
   All in the morning early.

My play-fellow in every sport,
   The moment I begin it ;
He 's always ready for a race,
   And always sure to win it.

At home, abroad, where'er I go,
   There Rover 's sure to be ;

There never was a kinder dog
  Than he has been to me.

My sister has a singing bird
  Within a cage of wire ;
My cousin George has every toy
  That children can desire ;

There 's Charley with his story-books, —
  He loves to read them over ;
There 's Edward has a rocking-horse,
  Whilst I have only Rover.

Dear Rover ! what care I for toys,
  Or birds of brilliant feather ?
Or books ! Come here, you little rogue,
  You 're worth them altogether.

THE BUTTERFLY.

Butterfly, butterfly, whither so fast ?
I 've followed you long — I must have you at last ;
    Butterfly, stop, I pray.
      " Oh, no, little maid,"
      The butterfly said,
    "Not a minute with you can I stay : —
Of the prettiest flowers I lift the lid,
I suck out the sweets that are under it hid,
    And then I am off and away."

Butterfly, butterfly, whither so high ?
I cannot talk to you up in the sky ;
    Come down with your painted wings fine ;
      Look, here is a pink,
      Just opened, I think,

The new drops all over it shine.
Dear butterfly, light on this flower a minute,
Believe me, the sweetest of honey is in it;
   Ah! butterfly — now you're mine!

ELIZABETH AND ISABEL.

I knew two little maidens once,
   I knew them very well,
And one was named Elizabeth,
   The other, Isabel.

Now, Lizzie was a docile child,
   And loved her mother dear;
But Isabel was obstinate :
   The story you shall hear.

It happened that these little girls
   Were taken ill one day;
They both were carried to their bed,
   And there, in pain, they lay.

Their tender mother, hoping she
   Might make her children well,

To Lizzie brought some medicine,
    The same to Isabel.

Lizzie, the good girl, swallowed it,
    Without a word to say ;
But Isabel still sobbed and cried,
    And pushed the spoon away.

More ill she grew by crying so,
    The foolish Isabel !
She would not take the medicine
    That might have made her well.

Elizabeth got better soon,
    And went to take a ride ;
But Isabel, the wilful girl,
    Grew worse — until she died !

MAMMA.

My own Mamma !
My dear Mamma !
How happy I shall be,
Tomorrow night,
At candle light,
When she comes home to me.

Tomorrow night,
At candle light,—
Yes, that's the time, they say,
That she   be here,
Our mother dear,
How long she's been away.

'T is just a week,
Since on my cheek

She pressed the parting kiss ;
   It seems like two,
   I never knew
So long a week as this.

   My tangled hair
   She smoothed with care,
With water bathed my brow ;
   And all with such
   A gentle touch —
There 's none to do so now.

   I cannot play
   When she 's away ;
There 's none to laugh with me ;
   And much I miss
   The tender kiss,—
The seat upon her knee.

When up to bed
I'm sorrowing led,
I linger on the stairs ;
I lie and weep—
I cannot sleep—
I scarce can say my prayers.

But she will come,
She'll be at home
Tomorrow night, and then
I hope that she
Will never be
So long away again.

TIED TO A CHAIR.

Against a chair poor puss was tied,
  Holding Georgiana's dolly;
Every now and then she cried
  With a mew and melancholy.

Georgiana's sister Lucy
  Trailing round her new broad chain,
Cried, "come, catch it, pretty pussy," —
  Pussy only mewed again.

Georgy laughed to hear her mew,
  Clapped her little hands, and cried
" Though you bid her play with you,
  Pussy cannot, *Pussy's tied.*"

"She must stand and hold my doll,
   And, to keep her steady there,
That she may not let it fall,
   I have tied her to the chair."

Hearing what her children said,
   Mamma soon set the pussy free;
Then Miss Georgy hung her head, —
   Lucy jumped about for glee.

"Georgy! now let's run away,"
   The merry little Lucy cried;
"Yes, my Lucy, you can play,
   But Georgy cannot — *Georgy's tied.*"

THE MOUSE.

Oh! little mouse, don't run away,
　I 'll use you well — I 'll give you food;
You need not be afraid to stay,
　I would not hurt you, if I could.

How cunning is your bright black eye,
　Your soft grey ears so silky, too,
I wish you would not be so shy,
　For I should like to play with you.

Come, you shall be my pretty pet,
　But do not struggle so, nor fear;
For you no wicked trap is set,
　And I 'm no pussy-cat, my dear.

I'll get you crumbs of cheese to eat,
   This little box your house shall be,
And you shall nibble sugar sweet,
   If you will only stay with me.

I have a little carriage fine,
   All painted green — 't is made of tin ;
If you will promise to be mine,
   Dear mouse, I 'll have you tackled in.

You will not ? — Ah! perhaps at home,
   Brothers and sisters, nine or ten,
Are waiting now for you to come,
   And you must make haste back again.

But pray take heed of what you do,
   Or puss will have you by the ear ;
She 's long been on the watch for you,
   And she can smell as well as hear.

Besides, 1 saw a trap to-day —
   It stands upon the pantry shelf;
I hope, if you should pass that way,
   You will be careful of yourself.

But you 're in haste, I see, to go,
   To keep you, then, I will not try;
So do not stare and tremble so,
   Poor, pretty little mouse — good-by.

B

THE BOY AND THE ROBIN.

'T is the pleasant month of June,
Roses will be blooming soon :
Sweetest month for rural play,
Sweeter than the earlier May.
Here 's a bank all mossy, green,
Bluer violets ne'er were seen ;
Here 's a handful — here 's another —
Tie them in a bunch for mother.
See the yellow butterfly,
But a moment does he lie
On the flower, or on the spray,
Stirs his wings and flits away.
See the Robin-red-breast ! how
He sits tilting on the bough.
" Robin, that 's a pretty seat
Where you sing so blithe and sweet,

Very pleasant it must be,
Sitting in the shady tree.
Oh! I wish that I were now
Tilting with you on that bough."
Thus it was the boy was heard
Gaily talking to the bird.
Robin turned his head aside,
And the urchin slyly eyed.
" Yes, my little master, gay " —
Twittering, thus he seemed to say;
" Yes, — but when the sun was gone,
And the starry night come on,
Little boy would find no nest,
Where to gather to his rest ;
Down, in vain, he 'd try to clamber,
Thinking of his bed and chamber ;
When the night winds shook the tree,
He with fear would shaken be.

B2

Tilting on the blossomed bough,
Scarce would seem so sweet as now;
And he would not like, a bit,
In the shady tree to sit;
We should hear him crying, then,
Take, O take me down again.

LUCY.

Lucy, what a pleasant day !
Shall we work, or shall we play ?
Work and play both make us glad,
Idleness alone is bad.

See the field flowers, how they grow ;
Hear the winds, how brisk they blow ;
See the Blue-bird build his nest ;
Nothing — nothing is at rest.

Like a little child at play,
Fast the small brook runs away,
And the gray clouds in the sky
Change their shapes and hurry by.

Bees are humming in and out;
Butterflies are all about;
Merry birds are on the wing;
Bubbles sparkle at the spring.

Bird and insect, flower and tree,
Know they must not idle be;
Each has something it must do,
Little Lucy, so must you.

FOR THE NEW YEAR.

I 've seen a rose-bush fading,
Its leaves were falling fast,
   It seemed to say
   " Alas ! the day !
My flowering time is past."

But shortly will the time come,
· When roses bloom again,
   And not a flower
   In summer's bower
Shall glow more brightly then.

I 've seen a little violet,
And this it seemed to say :

" My bloom is gone,
  I 'm all forlorn,
And withering away.

But in that pleasant season,
When winter nights are done,
    All gemmed with dew,
    My flowerets blue
Shall open to the sun."

Upon a leafless fruit-tree
I saw a Robin sit ;
    He seemed to wear
    A downcast air,
And chirped " te-whit, te-whit "

" Adieu ! " he said, " fair village,
Where I have lived so long ;

I 'll be this way
Some sweet spring day,
And sing a blither song."

I saw a lovely infant
Just sinking to his rest ;
His cheek of rose,
In soft repose,
Upon his mother's breast.

But soon, his slumber over,
A fairer sight than this,
With motion fleet,
He springs to meet
His mother's playful kiss.

I met a little maiden,
Her face was fair to see ;

D3

Her step was light,
Her eye was bright,
And this she said to me:

"The flowers have each their season,
All things their time to shine,
With vigor new,
And beauty too —
Why should not I have mine?

The time has come for me too,
New powers within to find;
NEW YEAR shall be
That time to me,
The spring-time of the mind.

A, B, C.

" Why must I learn my A, B, C ? "
Asked little Kate, " it wearies me ;
I wish to put my book away,
I wish to run about and play.
There 's kitty in the portico,
Oh dear ! if I could only go ;
Indeed, I think it very wrong
To make poor kitty wait so long ;
I 'll gather pretty flowers for you,
If I may go — do let me, do."

" Put by the book, my little maid,
You may go play," her mother said ;
" But when good little girls come here,
Who have been taught to read, my dear,

For them 't will very pleasant be
To read these story books to me ;
But you 'll not wish to stay with us,
You 'd rather go and play with puss."

" Nay, dear mamma, that must not be,
I 'll try to learn the A, B, C ;
But when I 've read my lesson, then
May I go play with puss again ? "

THE FLY.

A very little child, one day,
Picked a poor fly up, as it lay
   Upon the window seat ;
Stretched on his back, she saw him there,
His wings were stiff—and up in air
   Stiff stood his little feet.

She called her sister—"come, O come !"
And 'twixt her finger and her thumb
   She held him up to view.
"I wish, dear sister, you and I
Could find a little doctor fly
   To cure him !—do not you ? "

MISS NELLY.

Little Miss Nelly, in muslin and lace,
Sits up in the parlor with simpering face,
With frock of gay silk, and her ribbons of green,
And the prettiest slippers that ever were seen.
She fans herself gently, and sits on a chair,
And holds herself up with a womanly air.
In my calico frock, and my stout leather shoe,
I love to run out in the fields — do not you?

ELLEN TO HER COUSIN ANNA.

BY MRS. OSGOOD.

They tell me, love, that far away,
    Beyond the unfathomed tide,
I have a little friend at play,
    My grandsire's knee beside.

They bid me call her " cousin," dear,
    Her name is Anna Wells ;
And many a pretty tale of her
    My loving mother tells.

She says her lip is like a rose,
    Her eye a gem of light,
Her cheek such changing color shows,
    As veils the morning bright.

That o'er a forehead fair and mild
  Her soft brown hair is parted ;
And she 's a pleasant, playful child,
  A bright and happy-hearted.

Of one thing I am certain, dear,
  This dark-eyed coz must be
A lovely one, for oft I hear
  'That she resembles me.

And I, I do assure you, sweet,
  Am quite a perfect creature ;
Such dainty hands ! such cunning feet !
  Such grace of form and feature !

Rich, violet eyes, and auburn hair,
  A soft and pure complexion ;
And then, the lovely clothes I wear !
  They fit me to perfection.

I fear you 'll think me very vain,
   But, really, when I hear
My father talk in such a strain,
   How can I help it, dear ?

Sometimes, when in my cradle, I,
   In meditation meek,
Allow my silken lash to lie
   Demurely on my cheek —

He thinks that I am fast asleep,
   And bids mamma come near ;
While such a sober face I keep,
   He does not dream I hear.

" She 's really very beautiful,"
   This morn he, whispering, said ;
" How gracefully upon her breast
   Those tiny hands are laid !

There 's mind already on that brow,
  How bright the child is growing! .
Why, one would think she heard me now,
  She looks so very knowing!

Would you believe it? yesterday
  I chanced to breathe a sigh;
She looked directly in my face,
  And then began to cry!

Her reasoning powers are very strong —
  "Behold that bump!" he said;
(Don't tell! — it was a bump I got
  When mother knocked my head!)

Not he alone, but others, while
  My fond papa is by,
Declare I have the sweetest smile,
  The loveliest lip and eye!

They kiss, they hug, they toss me up,
   And do make such a pother ;
"The pretty little darling dear !
   The image of her mother ! "

But if papa but turns his eye,
   Or leaves me in their arms,
Why, in their arms they let me lie,
   Unheeding then my charms.

Ah ! cousin dear, experience
   Has taught me how to prize
The flattery of the faithless crowd
   Who laud my lips and eyes ;

And I have learned with stoic smile
   And brow serene, to hear,
Whene'er they choose to praise and pet
   "The little darling dear."

But these are trifles ; I have woes
  ' T will grieve thy loving heart
To hear, and in those radiant eyes
  The pitying tear will start !

Then listen, love, but breathe it not !
  I would not that the gay
And heartless world should know my lot, —
  And thou wilt not betray ?

In truth, to other's eyes I seem
  A tranquil child, and blest,
And none, not e'en mamma doth dream
  The sorrows of my breast !

The cheek may glow, the eye may smile,
  The lips in laughter part,
While coldly 'neath them all the while
  Slow throbs the suffering heart !

And first — (I know the child is blamed
    Whoe'er a parent blames ;
But who such trial tamely bears ?)
    My father calls me names !

Last night he dipped me, head and all,
    The naughty, cruel man !
And just because I chanced to fall,
    He called me " Pitch-a-pan ! "

And then, when struggling for my food,
    (I 'd been three hours without,)
And could not find it quick enough,
    ' T was little " Bob-about ! "

Mamma, too, when she takes me up,
    To fondle me begins,
And calls me " cherub," " snow-drop," " star ! "
    I can't think what she means !

What is a star? — Do you know, love?
  This morn, when on mamma
I smiled, — the nurse exclaimed, "she's wok
  As smiling as a star!"

This is not all, — whenever I
  (I can't do well without it,)
Think to enjoy a quiet cry,
  There's such a fuss about it!

The "luxury of tears" we all
  Have read in poet's dreams;
'T is left for babes like us to tell
  The luxury of "screams."

But scarce do hapless I begin,
  Than all are crowding round me,
And pull and push to find the pin
  With which my nurse has bound me.

Yet, when the pin does really prick,
  And I begin to whimper,
To cry and struggle, scream and kick,
  'T is " goodness ! what a temper ! "

Ah ! should I pain that gentle breast
  With all my infant troubles,
You 'd own that hope 's a dream, at best,
  And pleasures are but bubbles !

E'en now, to think of all my woe,
  My baby-heart is swelling;
But you will sympathize, I know,
  And love your cousin   ELLEN.

P. S.   And, dearest, when again you play
      Beside our grandpa's knee,
    Remember one who 's far away,
      And talk to him of me.

ANNA'S ANSWER TO HER COUSIN ELLEN.

Dear Ellen, when at first I heard
   About you from my mother,
With wishes warm my heart was stirred
   That we might know each other.

In many an hour of silent thought,
   My books and toys forgot,
Your name was to my memory brought,
   Although I knew you not.

At length your letter came; I felt
   Then in my bosom move
Something that seemed my heart to melt;
   Perhaps 't was *kindred love.*

And ever since, I think of you
   As one 'twixt whom and me
There should be gentle bonds, and true,
   Love, faith, and sympathy.

I often wish that in my arms
   I might awhile enfold you,
And gaze upon your infant charms—
   How carefully I 'd hold you.

So gently I would rock you, dear,—
   I 'd sing my sweetest songs,
And breathe them softly in your ear,
   That they might soothe your wrongs.

For, Ellen, I 've a tender heart,
   And sympathize I do,
And take a deep and feeling part
   In all that troubles you.

The lot of babes is hard, I know,
  The slaves to others' will ; —
Still to be dandled to and fro,
  And tossed and dandled still.

Before you know a word that 's said
  They 'll wisely bid you *talk*,
And while to stand you 're yet afraid,
  They 'll say the child can *walk*.

But, cousin, take your heart's delight,
  These are but trifles now ;
School days will come, — ah ! luckless wight, —
  Care then will cloud your brow.

Of school but little do I know,
  I 've only been one quarter ;
But I am sure I always go
  Like lamb led to the slaughter.

They tell of childhood's happy day ;
  Grown people talk about it,
When study was as sweet as play, —
  I hear the tale, and scout it.

Study soon wearies ; yet I know
  School books *do* make one clever ;
But play, — oh ! when you older grow,
  You 'll want to play forever.

To needle-work I 'm quite averse, —
  At hemming I rebel ;
My sewing up is something worse,
  And I do hate to *fell.*

A little history I know, —
  Stories I love to read ;
But writing copies fine and slow
  Is very hard indeed.

c2

Geography, — except the maps, —
  Is absolute vexation ;
And as to spelling ! oh, the traps,
  The deep mystification !

To play with lightsome step I go,
  Breezes and sunbeams round me ;
At school what pleasure can I know ?
  Four ugly walls to bound me !

There oft, on narrow bench, for hours
  I sit, till dreams steal o'er me,
Thinking far more of birds and flowers
  Than of the book before me.

Then in wrapt fancy o'er me crowd
  Fields, gardens, puss, and Tray ; —
Once I forgot, and *laughed aloud* ;
  Ah, well remembered day !

Then, swelling with indignant pride,
   I went, the live-long morning,
In corner dark my shame to hide,—
   To all an awful warning.

O'erwhelmed with woe, I took my stand
   Amid a silence solemn;
My dog-eared book held fast in hand,
   A tear on every column.

But let me, love, no more delay
   On such a theme of sorrow;
Though there be clouds and rain today,
   The sun may shine tomorrow.

And pray have patience, if you can;
   Your grief—I fain would quell it;
They'd better call you " Pitch-a-pan,"
   Than call you up to *spell it*.

     c2°

And when they name you " Bob-about,"
 Bear it — and think of her
Who, when she 'd bob or in or out,
 Is not allowed to stir.

You say your mother calls you " star : "
 'T is time that you should know,
Not only what those bright things are,
 But why she calls you so.

Some night, when all are fast asleep,
 Just raise your " violet eyes,"
And slyly through the curtains peep —
 You 'll see them in the skies.

You 'll see them glittering far and near,
 You 'll see them twinkling, blinking ; —
But gaze right on, and do not fear,
 'T is not at you they 're winking.

Though some do hold that from the sky
   They bend a little nearer,
Meeting a sinless infant's eye,
   And seem to shine out clearer.

Among those stars, so far outspread,
   Are some we planets call ;
And they are worlds like ours, 't is said —
   Don't start, dear, they wont fall.

Now all those pretty worlds are filled,
   I think, with babes like you ;
And you were from a star distilled,
   And thence they *name* you too.

Nick-names are vulgar things, but then
   'T is vulgar, too, to pout ;
So, if she calls you " star " again,
   Just blow the candles out.

I used to love your mother well ;
   And many an hour of glee,
And many a pleasant story-tell
   Has she enjoyed with me.

For me unnumbered toys she made,
   And oft my name would call ;
Sweet kisses on my lip she laid,
   And loved me best of all.

She sent me letters from afar,
   And baby verses too,
And dolls all dressed — your dear mamma !
   I wish she would send *you.*

But farewell now — heaven speed the time
   We shall together be,
When you to grandpa's arms shall climb,
   And I 'll sit on his knee.

'Till then sweet peace with you abide ;
　　Be patient, gentle, good ;
See life upon its sunniest side,
　　As *star-born spirits* should.

'T is far, 't is far across the sea,
　　But come and I will tell
What mirthful hours for you and me
　　Are held in store. — Farewell.

THE FLY AND THE RAIN-DROP.

One warm summer morning,
  A very small fly
Was dancing and buzzing
  All round in the sky.

"See!" says the little fly,
  "What I can do!
While I dance on my wings
  I can sing with them too."

From a cloud that was passing by,
  Fell a rain-drop,
And swallowed the poor little
  Buzzing fly up.

"Oh!" says the little fly,
  "What shall I do?
This is the strangest thing
  Ever I knew."

The thunder cloud burst
  And came down in a shower,
And the drop with the fly in it
  Fell on a flower.

"Oh!" says the little fly,
  "What shall I do?
I should be as well off
  With no wings as with two!"

The flower grew low
  By the side of a brook,
And into its waters
  The rain-drop she shook.

" Oh!" says the little fly,
  " What shall I do?
My wings and my body
  Are wet through and through."

Away ran the little brook,
  Faster than ever,
And tumbled the fly and drop
  Into the river.

" Oh!" says the little fly,
  " What shall I do?
Where am I going?
  I wish that I knew."

The river rolled on,
  With a mighty commotion,
And emptied the little drop
  Into the ocean.

" Oh ! " says the little fly,
  " What shall I do ?
The world is all turned
  Into water — 'tis true."

There came a great fish,
  With a fierce looking eye,
And he snapped at the drop
  For the sake of the fly.

" Oh!" says the little fly,
  " What shall we do ?
If the fish swallows you
  He will swallow me too."

But a sunbeam, that saw
  What the matter was there,
Drank the drop,
  And the fly was as free as the air.

    D

"Now," says the little fly,
    "See what I'll do!"
So he shook his little wings,
    And away he flew.

THE STORY OF LITTLE SARAH
AND
HER GRANDMOTHER'S JOHNNY-CAKE.

Little Sarah she stood by her grandmother's bed,
" And what shall I get for your breakfast ? " she
     said ;
" You shall get me a johnny-cake : quickly go
     make it,
In one minute mix, and in two minutes bake it."

So Sarah she went to the closet to see
If yet any meal in the barrel might be.
The barrel had long time been empty as wind ;
Not a speck of the bright yellow meal could she
     find.

But grandmother's johnny-cake — still she must
  make it;
In one minute mix, and in two minutes bake it.

She ran to the shop; but the shopkeeper said
" I have none — you must go to the miller, fair
  maid;
" For he has a mill, and he 'll put the corn in it,
And grind you some nice yellow meal in a
  minute; ·
But run, or the johnny-cake, how will you
  make it,
In one minute mix, and in two minutes bake it."

Then Sarah she run every step of the way,
But the miller said " no, I have no meal today;
Run, quick, to the corn-field, just over the hill,
And if any be there you may fetch it to mill.

Run, run, or the johnny-cake, how will you
    make it,
In one minute mix, and in two minutes bake it ? "

She ran to the corn-field — the corn had not
    grown,
Though the sun in the blue sky all pleasantly
    shone.
" Pretty sun," cried the maiden, " please make
    the corn grow ; "
" Pretty maid," the sun answered, " I cannot do
    so."
" Then grandmother's johnny-cake — how shall
    I make it,
In one minute mix, and in two minutes bake it ! "

Then Sarah looked round, and she saw what
    was wanted ;
The corn could not grow, for no corn had been
    planted.

She asked of the farmer to sow her some
    grain,
But the farmer he laughed till his sides ached
    again."
"Ho! ho! for the johnny-cake—how can you
    make it,
In one minute mix, and in two minutes bake
    it?"

The farmer he laughed, and he laughed out
    aloud,—
"And how can I plant till the earth has been
    ploughed?
Run, run to the ploughman, and bring him with
    speed,
He'll plough up the ground and I'll fill it with
    seed."
Away, then, ran Sarah, still hoping to make it,
In one minute mix, and in two minutes bake it.

The ploughman hé ploughed, and the grain it
    was sown,
And the sun shed his rays till the corn was all
    grown ;
It was ground at the mill, and again in her bed
These words to poor Sarah the grandmother
    said :
" You shall get me a johnny-cake — quickly go
    make it,
In one minute mix it, and in two minutes bake
    it."

CPSIA information can be obtained
at www.ICGtesting.com
Printed in the USA
LVOW11*2347050618
579656LV00013BA/339/P